Workbook Series

WORKING
THE
TRAIL

WORKING THE TRAIL

by Bill Topp, Editor and Keith Zirbel, Assistant Editor, *Referee* magazine

Graphics and layout by Matt Bowen, Graphic Designer, *Referee* magazine

Copyright © 2002 by Referee Enterprises, Inc., P.O. Box 161, Franksville, Wis. 53126.

Printed in the United States of America

ISBN 1-58208-033-X

Table of Contents

Introduction

When heading into a ball game, sometimes you need a quick review. *Working the Trail — Two-Person Mechanics* is designed to give you just that. It is the second of two books (the other being *Working the Lead — Two-Person Mechanics*) in a new *Referee* book line called "The Workbook Series." Other workbooks are planned for other sports.

The workbooks dissect details of specific officiating positions and give you an everything-you-ever-wanted-to-know flavor for that position. *Working the Trail* is based on the highly-successful *Referee* book, *Basketball Officials Guidebook for a Crew of Two Officials*. Within its 350-plus pages, the *Guidebook* covers mechanics from A to Z. For *Working the Trail*, we've used some of the best material from the *Guidebook*, plus added more quick tips, articles, graphics and even threw in some advice from top-notch officials — all specific to working the trail position. It compliments the *Guidebook* well.

This workbook will be a must-have for any new official, will serve as excellent meeting and camp and clinic material, and will be a great primer for any veteran heading into the season.

Special thanks to those who helped put this together, including those well-known officials who supplied us with the teaching tips within these pages. Real advice from really successful officials. Credit goes to Keith Zirbel, *Referee* assistant editor and a 10-year high school basketball official, and Matt Bowen, *Referee* publication design manager, for their hard work and creativity.

As with any of our book projects, we want to know what you think. Let us know your thoughts; they shape our future book decisions.

One of the lessons reinforced in this workbook is "stay in your primary," meaning stay focused on a specific task. Do the same with this workbook. Stay focused on what the trail does — and why — and your officiating will improve.

— Bill Topp, *Referee* editor

Think 'Trail'

The trail official must move aggressively, gain proper angles and work with the lead official to be successful.

> **Focus on your primary coverage area.** Conducting a thorough pregame will help define primary coverage areas and get the officials on the same wave length for the game.

> Work the arc. **Follow the arc forward on every shot** to monitor rebounding play and goaltending.

> Get on the same page with your partner. From the proper position, there are things **the trail can see more clearly than the lead.**

> **Don't be afraid to get beat** on the fast break. You will get beat occationally.

> **Be aware of the clock(s).** Keep refereeing until the period ends.

> Be prepared to **listen to the benches.** Listening is especially important in the closing seconds of a period when timeout requests may be frequent and critically timed.

> Be alert for problems at the table. **Know whether the arrow is correct,** manages substitutions efficiently and handles any questions from the table.

> Keep an eye on the play in transition. **Look over your shoulder as you run.** Resist the temptation to run backwards.

CHECK LIST

✔ Don't back pedal

✔ Stay in your primary

✔ Watch the clock

✔ Give strong signals

Penetrate toward the foul and make a strong signal.

0-20 PHOTOGRAPHIC

11 Ways to Become a Super Trail Official

The trail in a two person crew has a big job. Most of the time the trail is responsible for covering the play in three-quarters of the frontcourt, most three-point trys, helps out on rebounding fouls and violations and gets down court to cover the fast break.

We are all familiar with trail officials who stand at the division line and fade toward the other end when a shot goes up, leaving their partner to referee the scramble for the rebound. To get to be a "Super-T" get in these good habits.

1. Focus on your primary coverage area. The ball is a magnet for the eyes. Super-T knows when to focus off the ball and trusts his or her partner. Conducting a thorough pregame will help define primary coverage areas and get the officials on the same wave length for the game.

2. Work the arc. The three point shot added to the trail's responsibilities. However, the segment of the arc between the free-throw line extended and the top of the key provides guidance for the trail's movements. Super-T will follow the arc forward on every shot to monitor rebounding play and goaltending. To cover a three-point try from the other side of the lane, Super-T will follow the arc to the top of the key. Super-T will *always* move to look between the offense and the defense and will stay with the shooter until the shooter is back to the floor. Super-T will penalize the aggressive box out and not be fooled by the flop.

There is one time when the trail must abandon the arc. To referee a trap on the far side of the court near the division line, Super-T will go back toward the center circle, even into the backcourt, to get an angle on the play.

3. Get on the same page with your partner. Some lead officials are sensitive when the trail calls something under the hoop. The really good ones just say, "Thanks for picking me up."

Hank Nichols, NCAA coordinator of men's basketball officiating, has often advised, "Don't pass on an obvious call." From the proper position, there are things the trail can see more clearly than the lead. Rebound fouls are one. The trail near the free-throw line extended can see whether there is a push or other illegal contact. The foot shuffle on the put back shot or a fast break layup is another trail priority, as is the push in the back of a dribbler. Reach an understanding with your partner that you will make calls you are 110 percent sure of. Always remember you can't look good unless your partner does too.

4. Don't be afraid to get beat on the fast break. That is the excuse given for standing on the division line when a shot goes up. Super-T does not mean super fast. You will get beat occasionally. Practice refereeing fast breaks from behind in some scrimmages. Slip toward the lane at about the free-throw line to see between the dribbler and the defender *and clear out quickly.*

5. Be aware of the clock(s). Referees get blamed for timing mistakes, so make it a point to see whether the clock stops and starts exactly as it should. Judge whether the horn is loud enough to hear on a last-second shot. See whether you can get into a position to see both the play and clock as the last seconds of a period tick down. Remember, the period does not end until the try is over even if the shot is a wild heave. Desperate defenders sometimes collide with desperate shooters after the horn. Keep refereeing until the period ends. On a last-second call, look at the clock immediately after the whistle. It should be stopped by then. Before administering foul shots with little time remaining, check the clock so you can correct the time if the clock starts erroneously.

In some games a two-person crew also has to deal with a shot clock. The biggest problem is an improper reset of the clock. Impress the clock operator with the idea the clock should not be reset at a whistle until it is certain it should be. Train yourself to glance at the shot clock after every call so that you know how much to put back if it is reset improperly. That takes practice.

BRIAN SPURLOCK

Try This

"Officiating is very much reactive. You react to the play and if it violates the spirit and intent of the rules, if it violates the guidelines, you blow the whistle."

— Mike Wood
NCAA Division I Men's Official

6. Be prepared to listen to the benches. The trail is usually the one the coach will be talking to. Listening is especially important in the closing seconds of a period when timeout requests may be frequent and critically timed. Super-T will identify the head coach's voice during the game so timeouts can be granted promptly at a key point. Anticipate the game situations when a timeout might be wanted.

Of course, other things get said to you as you go by the bench. Super-T will know the difference between complaint and abuse. Never tolerate abuse.

7. Be alert for problems at the table. Super-T knows whether the arrow is correct, manages substitutions efficiently and handles any questions from the table. Super-T knows when the bonus is imminent, where the timeouts stand and reminds the timer of last-second shot duties.

8. Keep an eye on the play in transition. In their anxiety to avoid getting beat down the court in transition, some officials just put their heads down and sprint from trail to lead. Sometimes, those officials will get to the end-line alone because an interception

QuickTip

Don't Play Dead During Downtime

Staying in the game while the ball is dead is crucial to an official. There are many different things you can do to "keep your head in the game." Communicating with your partner(s), recapping game info (score, quarter, who gets the ball where, etc.) and talking to players are some ways to keep focused. If circumstances allow for you to share a word with a player (as the PlayPic illustrates), why not do it? Having a short, general, game-related conversation doesn't allow your mind to wander. It also shows the players you're human and not an unruly authoritative figure. Just be sure if you talk with one team, try to talk with the other.

PlayPic™

occurred and play is back at the other end. Look over your shoulder as you run. Resist the temptation to run backwards. Collisions are painful for everyone.

Before starting from trail to lead, make sure there is no press to deal with. Some teams press after every score. Pay attention early in the game and be prepared to stay to help cover the play.

9. Stay in good position as the play comes up the court. As the new trail after a score or rebound, don't get ahead of the ball. Stay a step or two behind the ball and to one side. That will enable you to see between the ball handler and any defender. You will also be able to look ahead of ball to see any screens that might be set and referee any block/charge situations. Super-T will see the crash coming and stay with it to make the right judgment.

10. Head off three-point questions with clear signals. The trail must give the touchdown signal on every three-point goal, even if the lead makes the call in the far corner. On shots where the shooter's foot just touched the arc, it pays to signal two points about waist high so the table (and the coach) know you saw the play. In the rare situations in which your partner erroneously signals three,

blow the whistle and correct the call.

11. See the foot movements of the three-point shooter. Two things are common: a player gets the ball with a foot on the arc and moves both to get behind it; or the player catches the ball with one or both feet on the floor and moves both feet to gather for the shot. Both moves are travel violations. Call them.

It takes some work to become a Super-T, but it makes the game a lot better. Your partners will be thankful.

(Written by Bill Kenney, Florham, N.J.) □

2 Court Coverage

The trail must move off the sideline for proper court coverage. That allows the lead to watch players off-ball, the critical component to controlling physical play.

> The new **trail is responsible for the backcourt endline** and for the sideline opposite the new lead.

> The new **lead is responsible for the frontcourt endline.**

> *Referee* recommends that the **sideline opposite the trail in the backcourt is a shared responsibility.**

> The trail must **get off the sideline** to officiate those coverage areas correctly. It takes a lot of movement and an understanding of good angles. Proper coverage requires good eye contact and a "feel" for where your partner is looking.

> By correctly placing so much emphasis on off-ball coverage for the lead, **some boundary line coverage sometimes gets sacrificed.**

> There's a great **myth among referees that the lead is the only official who can call block/charge** near the lane. That's wrong.

> A one- or two-step move left or right **eliminates straightlining.**

CHECK LIST

✔ Watch the division line

✔ Cover the opposite sideline

✔ Stay behind the play

✔ Stay out of passing lanes

Look through the play as Pat Strong, Indianapolis, does here.

JIM WHITE

Court coverage: Basic Frontcourt Responsibilities (2-1)

In the frontcourt, basic coverage shifts depending on which official is on-ball.

In MechaniGram 2-1, the lead's on-ball responsibilities include the area below the free-throw line extended to the far edge of the free-throw lane line (away from the lead) when the lead is opposite the trail and the floor is balanced.

When the lead is on-ball, the trail's off-ball responsibilities include the area above the free-throw line extended to the division line and the lane area from the free-throw lane line (nearest the trail) to the sideline nearest the trail.

MechaniGram 2-1 illustrates basic guidelines for coverage. Specific officiating movements designed to better cover particular plays force the officials to adjust coverage. □

2-1

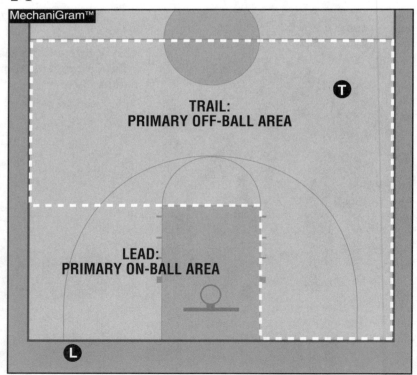

MechaniGram™

TRAIL:
PRIMARY OFF-BALL AREA

LEAD:
PRIMARY ON-BALL AREA

Boundary Coverage: Basic Frontcourt Responsibilities (2-2)

Covering boundary lines is among the most difficult tasks using a crew of two officials. By correctly placing so much emphasis on off-ball coverage for the lead, some boundary line coverage sometimes gets sacrificed.

The NFHS manual states that in the frontcourt the lead is responsible for the sideline nearest the lead and the endline. The trail is respon-sible for the division line and the sideline nearest the trail. While in theory that sounds easy, the actual practice is very difficult and sacri-fices off-ball coverage in the lane area.

Here's an example. A trouble spot for two-person crews is a play-er who has the ball near the side-line above the free-throw line extended and opposite the trail. The trail correctly moves toward the center of the court to officiate the action on the player with the ball, such as fouls, traveling viola-tions, etc.

2-2

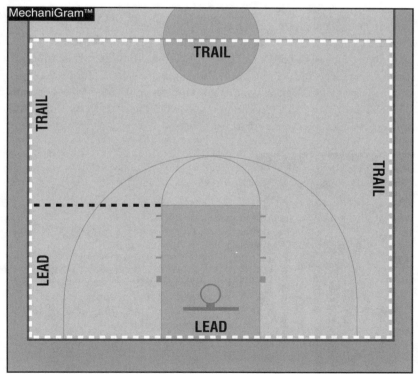

The problem: Manuals state that sideline is the lead's responsibility. Well, if the lead has to look beyond the free-throw line extended to watch for a potential sideline violation and the trail has to watch for fouls, etc., who is watching the other players? No one. There are too many off-ball problems that can occur if no one is supervising those players.

Referee recommends that the trail also have opposite sideline responsibility above the free-throw line extended. Sometimes, the trail must move well beyond the center of the court to see an out-of-bounds violation. Stay deep (toward the division line) on the play to get a good angle.

Though not the best sideline coverage, you're making a conscious sacrifice. You might occasionally miss an out-of-bounds call. Obviously, we don't want to miss calls. However, that's better than missing an off-ball elbow to a player's head because no one was watching. It's a trade-off we must make: Off-ball coverage to control rough physical play is more important than an occasional missed sideline violation. □

Split The Court On Drives To The Basket (2-3)

Sometimes, the lead doesn't have enough time to get ball side, avoid quicksand and get a good look on drives toward the basket. When players make quick passes away from the lead that cover a great distance, it's difficult to react in time to get a good angle.

When that happens, there's a simple solution: "You take the stuff on your side of the hoop and I'll take the stuff on my side of the hoop."

Try This

"When there is a three-point attempt in the gray area, there can only be one attempt signal. If there are two officials with signals, your off-ball coverage breaks down."

— Sally Bell
NCAA Division I Women's Official

There's a great myth among referees that the lead is the only official who can call block/charge near the lane. That's wrong. That attitude places too much pressure on the lead because there's too much to watch. It also leaves the lead straightlined and guessing on many plays that aren't on the lead's side of the floor.

When the lead is on the far side of the court, the trail has a much better look on drives to the lane that start on the trail's half of the court. But it takes an aggressive, hard-working trail to make the call correctly and with conviction.

As the trail, penetrate toward the endline to get the proper angle on the drive to basket. Referee the defense. Make the call. It's really that simple.

In MechaniGram 2-3, the officials start the play with the floor balanced. ② quickly passes to ①, who quickly passes to ③. ③ immediately drives around ③ toward the basket. The action is too fast for the lead to move ball side. As ③ drives toward the basket, ④ steps in to take a charge. The trail penetrates toward the endline, gets a good angle and makes the judgment on the contact. □

2-3

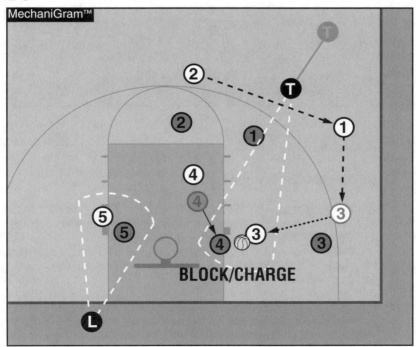

Court Coverage: Backcourt, No Defensive Pressure (2-4)

When play moves from one end-line toward the other, the trail has primary responsibility in the backcourt. For example, after a made basket the trail is responsible for the throw-in and watches the players move to the other end of the court.

In any transition effective coverage means significant movement by the trail. Similar to half-court coverage, the trail must move off the sideline. □

2-4

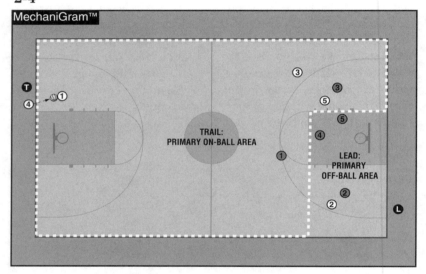

MechaniGram™

TRAIL:
PRIMARY ON-BALL AREA

LEAD:
PRIMARY
OFF-BALL AREA

QuickTip

Get the ball in play quickly

One of the great aspects of basketball is that the action is nearly non-stop. You can take advantage of that and help the game move along smoothly by getting the ball in play quickly after a stoppage.

When the ball is dead and little is happening on the court, it's prime-time for trouble. Players stop worrying about offensive plays and defensive schemes and start focusing on other players or the officials. The same is true for coaches. When the ball is dead they've got little to worry about and they often begin unnecessary conversations with opponents and officials.

When the ball is dead, get the ball back in play as quickly as possible without rushing or sacrificing duties. The faster the ball gets back in play, the quicker players and coaches return their focus to the game.

Straightlining (2-5)

"Straightlining" occurs when your view of a play is obstructed by the players themselves. In effect, you are in a straight line with the players and have no angle to see between them.

A one- or two-step move left or right eliminates straightlining. Keep your head up and continually watch the play when moving.

The most common straightlining concerns:

1. Offensive player with the ball with defensive pressure. You must avoid straightlining so that you can see between the players and correctly judge the play. Did the defender slap the dribbler's arm? Did the offensive player push off on the drive? Did the defender establish legal guarding position?

2. Low post play. To correctly officiate action around the low blocks — on-ball or off-ball — you must avoid straightlining. Coupled with proper spacing, you can judge whether or not the offensive player pushed off to receive the drop pass, the defender pushed the offensive post player in the lower back or if the offensive player hooked the defender on the spin move to the basket.

3. Screens. Get good angles to see screens. Avoid straightlining and you'll see if the screen was legally set, if the defender fouled while pushing through the screen or if the screener fouled by extended a leg, hip or elbow.

Those decisions and others are nearly impossible if you're straightlined.

PlayPics 2-5A and 2-5B show a play with the official's view. In PlayPic 2-5A, the official is straightlined. In PlayPic 2-5B, the official has a better angle. □

2-5A

Straightlined

2-5B

Good angle

3 The Trail: Where To Go

Angles are just as important as distance. Stay deep on plays to keep good angles and avoid being in passing lanes.

> When an offensive player has the ball opposite the trail, **the trail must move away from the closest sideline** and get proper angles.

> When moving toward the center of the court, the trail must **stay deep** (toward the division line) to avoid passing lanes.

> When a swing pass occurs with the trail in the middle of the court, the trail must **use an inside-out look;** a one- or two-step adjustment toward the center of the court gives you the proper angle.

> When a player takes a shot within the trail's coverage area, the trail's first responsibility is to **watch the airborne shooter** all the way back to the floor to ensure there are no offensive or defensive fouls.

> After a shot is taken, the trail must **penetrate toward the endline** to improve rebounding angles.

> The trail must **watch the area in the lane** when a post player spins away from the lead.

CHECK LIST

✔ Stay deep

✔ Get good angles

✔ Penetrate toward the endline

✔ Get the shooter to the floor

Stay a step or so behind the play as it crosses the division line, as high school referee Rich Porter does here.

BOB MESSINA

The 'Inside-out' Look (3-1)

With a crew of two officials, the trail official often has to get off the sideline and move toward the center of the court to officiate action on the far side of the floor. When that happens, the trail can get caught in the middle on a swing pass from one side of the court to the other. Adjustments must be made.

When a swing pass moves from the sideline opposite the trail across the top of the key to the near-side wing, the trail can get straightlined because of the position off the sideline. When a quick swing pass straightlines you and gives you a poor angle, you must make an adjustment to improve the angle.

A simple one- or two-step adjustment *toward the center of the court* gives you the proper angle., as in MechaniGram 3-1A. You must fight the urge to run around the entire play toward the sideline, using six steps or more and wasting precious time. By the time you run around the play, the offensive player could take a shot (was the shooter's foot on or behind the three-point arc?), violate or be fouled — and you may not have seen it.

3-1A

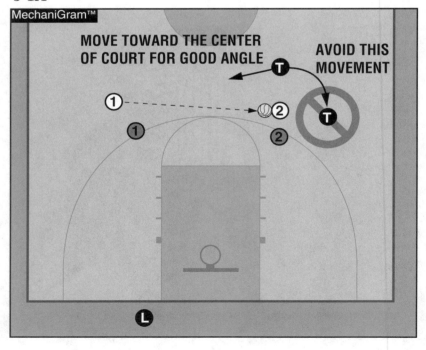

MechaniGram™

MOVE TOWARD THE CENTER OF COURT FOR GOOD ANGLE

AVOID THIS MOVEMENT

After adjusting one or two steps toward the center to improve your angle, watch the entire play from there, including a jump shot follow-through and landing. After you've taken care of that responsibility, you can move toward the sideline and endline, working for your next good angle on rebounding action.

In PlayPic 3-1B, the trail is straightlined on the play and must move to see potential contact on or by the shooter. In PlayPic 3-1C, the trail moves one or two steps toward the center of the court. From there, the trail has a great look at the defensive player lunging at the shooter.

You must fight the urge to run around the entire play toward your sideline, using six steps or more and wasting precious time. □

Trail Must Pick Up Shooter On Skip Pass (3-2)

Ball-side mechanics are effective for controlling post play. One weakness is coverage of a skip pass to the opposite wing player for a quick shot. A skip pass is a quick pass from one side of the floor to the other, designed to take advantage of a sagging defense. Taboo years ago, it's now seen at virtually every level.

If there is no quick shot and the lead can adjust back to the other side of the court without haste, the lead then picks up the ball (assuming it is below the free-throw line extended) and the trail moves back toward the sideline, getting good angles to watch off-

3-1B

From this set up

3-1C

Use this movement

ball. The lead must continue to watch off-ball in the lane area while moving until completely across the lane and in a good position to pick up the player with the ball.

In MechaniGram 3-2A, the lead has moved ball side. ① throws a skip pass to ③, who quickly shoots. Since the lead is ball side and doesn't have enough time to balance the floor, the trail picks up ③, even though ③ is below the free-throw line extended. The trail should penetrate slightly toward the play to improve the angle.

A good pregame conference and good eye contact during the game give you a better chance to officiate the skip pass correctly.

In PlayPic 3-2B, the trail is pri-mary on-ball, watching the perimeter player with the ball. The lead has moved ball side to watch post play. The perimeter player then throws a skip pass to a teammate near the opposite sideline. In PlayPic 3-2C, the trail adjusts toward the center of the court and picks up the shooter. The trail must help on that skip pass — even though the shooter is below the free-throw line extended — because the lead is ball side and does not have enough time to balance the floor.

After the shot is released, the trail watches the shooter return to the floor, looking for fouls, etc. Next, the trail penetrates toward the endline for improved rebounding angles. □

3-2A

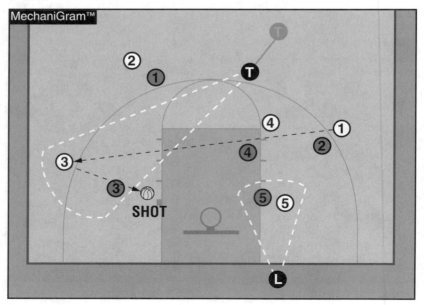

3-2B

3-2C

Trail Movement Off Sideline (3-3)

In MechaniGram 3-3A, ① with the ball is far away from the trail official — though the player is still the trail's responsibility —

and there's defensive pressure. To see the play well, the trail must move off the near sideline and work to get a good angle.

Avoid moving straight toward the play: You could interfere with the play by stepping into a passing lane. Take an angle toward

3-3A

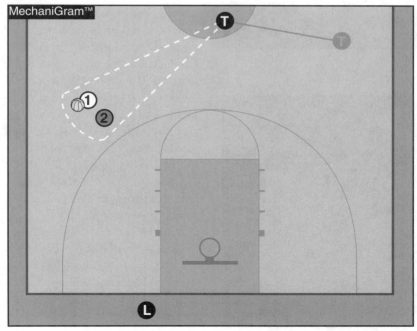

the division line to decrease your chances of interfering with the play. In extreme cases, you may even position yourself in the back-court.

By moving off the sideline and angling toward the backcourt, you're in a much better position to see the play.

3-3B

PlayPic™

3-3C

PlayPic™

Effective court coverage requires significant movement by the trail.

In PlayPic 3-3B, the player with the ball is near the sideline oppo-site the trail and above the free-throw line extended — still the trail's responsibility. The trail is too far away and must adjust toward the center of the court.

In PlayPic 3-3C, the trail adjusts toward the center of the court for the proper distance and angle. Notice the trail also stays deep to avoid passing lanes. □

Trail Looks Weak Side When Lead Moves Ball Side (3-4)

There are many benefits of the lead moving ball side for post action. One potential problem, however, is weak side rebounding action. With the lead on the same side of the floor as the trail, the lane area opposite both officials can present problems.

With the lead ball-side and already watching post play near the closest lane line, it is difficult for the lead to watch players away from that area in the lane. First, primary concentration is — and should be — on the post play. Second, it is difficult for the lead to see the opposite side of the lane because the lead is looking through lane congestion and is easily straightlined.

When the lead moves ball side, it is the trail's responsibility to observe weak side rebounding action. Though somewhat of a long-distance look, with the proper penetration toward the endline to get a good angle the trail can effectively watch weak side rebounding action.

In MechaniGram 3-4, the trail watches ③ deliver a drop pass to ⑤, who has effectively posted up on the low block. The lead already moved ball side anticipating the play. ⑤ seals off the defender and pivots strongly to the basket. The lead watches the post-up action.

Anticipating the play, the trail adjusts for a good angle and looks opposite. From that spot, the trail can look through the lane and watch ④ battle ④ on the weak side for rebounding positioning.

If you're the trail and you see a foul on the weak side, penetrate toward the lane and sell the call. By moving into the lane area aggressively (roughly around the intersection of the lane line and the free-throw line), the trail will cut the distance. Perception is important. If you look like you're close to the play and in good position, your ruling has a better chance of being accepted. ☐

3-4

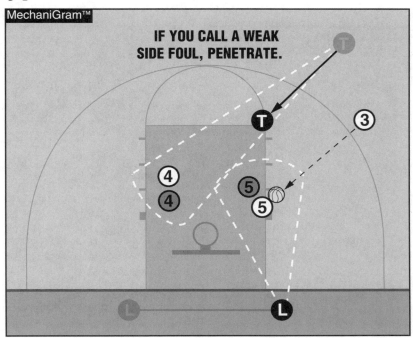

MechaniGram™

IF YOU CALL A WEAK
SIDE FOUL, PENETRATE.

Trail Must Work 'Backside' in Lane Area (3-5)

A trouble spot for the lead develops when a player with the ball on the low block spins toward the middle of the lane away from the lead. The quick spin move often leaves the lead straightlined and without a good look on the play.

Many times, a defender near the free-throw line will drop down into the lane and challenge the move toward the basket. That's when you'll likely see that defender slap at the offensive player, trying to poke the ball away. That

steal attempt is sometimes a foul — one that goes unseen by the now-straightlined lead.

The trail must help out and watch the area in the lane when a post player spins away from the lead. Commonly referred to as the lead's "backside," the trail has a much better look at the play after penetrating toward the endline for an improved angle.

In MechaniGram 3-5A, ③ has the ball on the low block in front of the lead. ③ then spins toward the middle of the lane and drives toward the basket.

② drops down and attempts the steal. The lead watches the post up action and the initial spin

3-5A

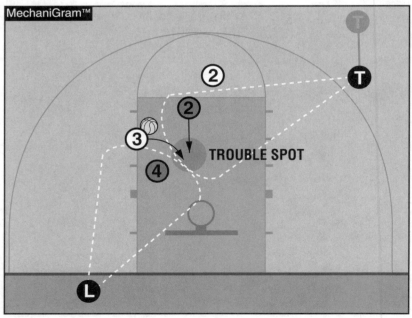

move. The trail penetrates toward the endline, gets a good angle and watches ② defend the play. The lead's backside is protected.

Come in strong and sell the call if you're the trail and you see a foul. Move toward the call to cut down the distance on the play. Perception is important. If you look like you're close to the play and in good position your ruling has a better chance of being accepted.

In PlayPic 3-5B, the lead is watching low post action. In PlayPic 3-5C, the offensive player spins away from the lead and a second defender moves toward the offensive player to attempt a steal — it's a congested, straightlined view for the lead.

PlayPic 3-5D illustrates the trail's excellent backside view as the second defender slaps the offensive player. That's the trail's call since the spin move went away from the lead. □

3-5B

3-5C

3-5D

Trail Movement on Jump Shot (3-6)

The trail has more responsibilities than simply watching the shooter. Too often a shot goes up and the trail's first thought is to start moving to the other end of the floor to avoid getting beat down court. When the trail leaves, the lead is left with offensive players crashing the boards and defensive players doing all they can to grab the rebound. That's too much for one person to handle.

The trail must help with rebounding action. When a player takes a jump shot within the trail's coverage area, the first responsibility is to watch the airborne shooter all the way back to the floor to ensure there are no offensive or defensive fouls (PlayPic 3-6A). While watching that action, the trail should be moving a couple of steps toward the endline (PlayPic 3-6B).

Once everything is OK with the shooter and surrounding action, the steps toward the endline allow the trail to help the lead by watching rebounding action. A step or two to improve your angle is all that's necessary to successfully watch rebounding action (PlayPic 3-6C). Avoid going below the free-throw line extended. The trail is likely to see an offensive player pushing (or crashing into) a defensive player

from behind — something that is difficult for the lead to see from the endline (PlayPic 3-6D).

Do the game, your partner and yourself a favor and resist the urge to sprint to the other end of the floor when the shot goes up. Move toward the endline to get rebounding angles. ☐

Judging Goaltending (3-7)

Goaltending is arguably one of the most difficult calls in basketball. It can get officials in trouble for a couple of reasons:

1. It doesn't happen very often (especially during high school and lower-level games).

2. Officials are usually not watching the ball after it has been released on a try.

In almost all situations, the trail is responsible for goaltending. However, the lead can call goaltending if the trail doesn't see it. That's *very* rare because the lead shouldn't be watching the flight of the ball from the endline; the lead should be watching strong-side rebounding, etc. Another exception: When the trail moving to new lead on a transition play is behind the fastbreak play, the new lead has primary goaltending responsibility.

Because goaltending is somewhat rare, it becomes a reactionary call that can take you by surprise. Too often the trail is correctly watching other things: fouls in the act of shooting, three-point lines, fouls after the try has been released, weak-side rebounding, etc. When a defensive player leaps

DALE BARNES

Try This

"The trail official should at all times maintain a position to the left or right of the ball. The position of outside in will enable the trail official to referee as many players as possible as well as on the ball coverage."

– Joe Forte, NBA Official

to block the shot, an official's reaction is sometimes just a bit slow, reducing judgment to guesswork.

The NFHS rule on goaltending reads, "Goaltending occurs when a player touches the ball during a field goal try or tap while:

a. The ball is in downward flight.

b. The entire ball is above the level of the basket ring.

c. The ball has a possibility of entering the basket in flight.

d. The ball is not touching an imaginary cylinder which has the basket ring as its lower base."

To correctly rule on goaltend-ing, you must judge the arc of the ball. That's easier said than done because of all the other things you have to observe. In theory it's simple: ball is upward, no-call; ball is downward, goaltending. The reality is much different, especially when the ball is near its apex, or the top of the arc. The short- to medium-range jump shots are most difficult, generally because they happen so quickly.

One simple tool officials can use to help themselves judge goal-tending correctly is knowing where the defender is in relation to the shooter and the basket.

3-7A   No call

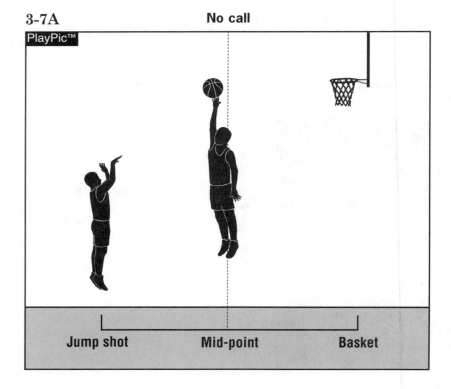

PlayPic™

| Jump shot | Mid-point | Basket |

Simply stated, if the defender is closer to the shooter than to the basket when the ball is touched, you've likely got a no-call because the ball is likely still on its way up (PlayPic 3-7A). If the defender is closer to the basket than to the shooter when the ball is touched, it's probably goaltending because the ball is likely on its way down (PlayPic 3-7B).

Understand that advice is merely a *guideline* to help officials, it is not a cure-all. Judging goaltending still requires a knowledge of where the ball was touched in its arc, but knowing where the defender was when the ball was touched can help when making that tough call or no-call. □

Basketball Basics: Pinching In (3-8)

When working as a trail official, one helpful mechanic is the "pinch."

As a trail official who is watching a perimeter player with the ball, be ready to respond if the player takes a shot. There's a natural tendency to either stand still or move toward the other end of

3-7B   **Goaltending**

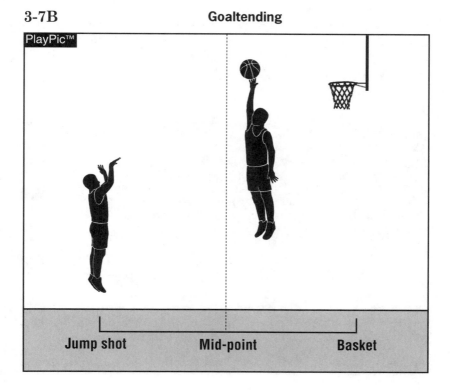

Jump shot   Mid-point   Basket

the floor, anticipating a fast break. Fight that tendency by pinching in on the play. Here's how it works:

Focus on the jump shooter in your area. Watch the player as he is airborne, until he returns to the floor and it is clear there is neither an offensive or defensive foul. While your eyes are focused in the shooter's area, take one or two steps toward the baseline, "pinching" in to get the best possible angle on rebounders. For example, if you start the play at the top of the key, you end up at about the free-throw line extended.

After you've determined there are no fouls involving the shooter and you've pinched in, you're in a better position to shift your eyes to the rebounders. Be especially mindful of the offensive rebounder crashing the boards through

defenders. That's a tough call for the lead official to make; the trail, after pinching in, generally has a much better look at that play. Don't worry too much about getting beat at the other end; you're more valuable pinching in and looking at rebounders than standing at half court leaving your partner to take care of all rebounding action. ☐

Spacing For The Trail (3-9)

Officiating with a crew of two officials requires a lot of movement. That movement offers better court coverage, but sometimes the movements of the official and the players cause the official to be too close to the action.

3-8

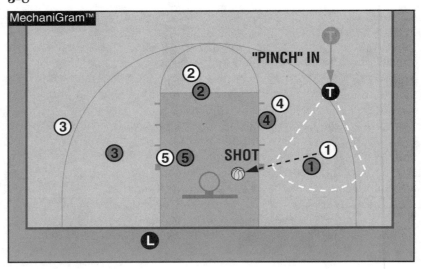

"Spacing" is the distance between you and the play. If you're too close or too far, you can't see the play clearly.

When you get too close to a play, your view of the play is distorted. Your depth perception is off and your field of vision is narrow. It's kind of like reading this book when it's two inches from your nose vs. at normal reading length. You can see it a lot better when it's further away from your face. The same principles hold true on the court. Also, if you're too close, you're more likely to get in the way by colliding with players or being in passing lanes. You risk impacting the play or causing injuries to the players and yourself.

If you're too far, you're not in position to see the play. This time it's like reading a book that is across the room. Even if you could see the play clearly, you're not going to be able to convince anyone you did see the play right when you're so far away. The perception is that you were too far away to see it.

What's the right distance for the trail? It depends on where the play is. If the play is in the immediate area, position yourself around 10-15 feet from the play. If the play is closer to the far sideline, 20-25 feet, depending on defensive pressure. With more pressure, 15-20 feet. Those distances are only guidelines. Ultimately, you want to be close enough to give the perception you can see the play from where you are and far enough to keep the proper perspective and stay out of the way.

In PlayPic 3-9A, the trail is too close. In PlayPic 3-9B, the trail creates proper spacing by backing up. □

3-9A

Too close

3-9B

Good spacing

Free Throws

Adjust your angles as a trail to properly cover the free-throw action.

> The trail is always positioned **facing the scorer's table.**

> The trail is positioned at a spot just **behind the free-throw line extended** halfway between the trail-side lane line and the trail-side sideline. Many officials incorrectly back up all the way to the sideline; it's impossible to correctly watch the players on the opposite lane line from there.

> Do not take a spot even with the free-throw line extended; **move about one or two strides toward the division line.** That angle allows you to clearly see the free thrower and the opposite lane line.

> **Do not step into the lane;** the lead administers the free throw alone.

> After the free thrower has caught the ball from the lead, **pick up the visible 10-second count** with the arm farthest from the basket.

> Immediately after the free thrower releases the shot, use the "do not start clock" signal with open hand raised directly above your head. **Use the arm farthest from the basket** so the timer sees the signal.

> During the flight of the try and with your arm still raised, **penetrate slightly toward the endline** using a two-step crossover move. That movement ensures good angles on rebounding action.

CHECK LIST

✔ Face the table

✔ Watch cross court

✔ Stay off the sideline

✔ Penetrate on the shot

Count with your outside hand, as Lucy Nalin, Carmel, Ind., does here.

DALE GARVEY

Trail positioning

The trail has a specific spot to ensure proper coverage.

• The trail is always positioned facing the scorer's table.

• The trail is positioned at a spot just behind the free-throw line extended halfway between the trail-side lane line and the trail-side sideline. Many officials incorrectly back up all the way to the sideline; it's impossible to correctly watch the players on the opposite lane line from there.

• Do not take a spot even with the free-throw line extended; move about one or two strides toward the division line. That angle allows you to clearly see the free thrower and the opposite lane line.

The only exception to that position is technical foul administration.

Trail movements

The trail has specific movements during free throws.

• Do not step into the lane; the lead administers the free throw alone.

• Maintain normal trail free-throw position.

• After the free thrower has caught the ball from the lead, pick up the visible 10-second count with the arm farthest from the basket.

• Immediately after the free thrower releases the shot, use the "do not start clock" signal with open hand raised directly above

BRIAN SPURLOCK

Try This

"The trail isn't the administering official on a technical foul, so if there's any question regarding the administration of the technical foul from the scorer's table, you need to be aware what type of technical it was to be able to help the table."

– John Clougherty
NCAA Division I Men's Official

your head. Use the arm farthest from the basket so the timer sees the signal.

• During the flight of the try and with your arm still raised, penetrate slightly toward the end-line using a two-step crossover move. That movement ensures good angles on rebounding action.

• If the shot is good, lower your arm. There is no need to signal a made free throw.

• If the shot is no good and the ball is to remain live, use the "start the clock" signal as soon as the ball touches or is touched by a player.

Since the trail is always facing the scorer's table, the trail must

be aware of reporting substitutes. If a sub is entering between free throws, tell the lead to wait to administer the final free throw until the substitution is complete. □

Technical Foul Administration (4-1)

Technical foul administration is one area of coverage where things seem to vary greatly in different state and local associations and different leagues.

For NFHS mechanics, the two officials switch on the technical foul, just as they would with any

4-1

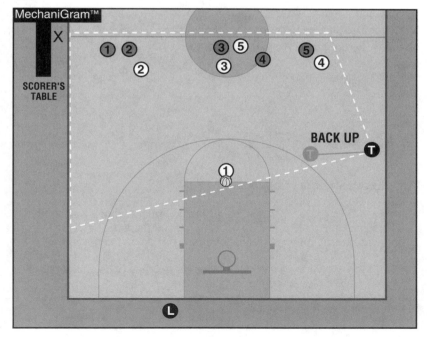

foul. Technical foul free throws are administered in the same manner as other free throws.

The NFHS manual also states, "If the situation requires, the lead official may administer both free throws while the trail official moves to a position which provides maximum supervision." That's sound advice because during technical foul free throws, often players bunch up near the division line. Since technical fouls are usually emotional in nature, there could be lingering problems among players.

Referee recommendation: If the technical foul was called on a player who did something unsportsmanlike toward an opponent and those players remain on the floor during the free throws, let the lead administer the free throws alone while the trail moves toward the division line to watch those players. Having a presence near the division line may be enough to stop the problem.

When the trail remains near the free-throw line during administration, back up farther toward the sideline than you normally would to ensure you see all players near the division line. There's no need to be in tight like during a normal free throw because there are no players lined up along the lane line to watch. The trail's primary responsibility is the remaining nine players and the benches; secondary responsibility is the free thrower. You're simply playing the odds. You're more likely to have problems among the other players or the benches than you are to have a violation on the free thrower.

QuickTip

Leave the court quickly

There's an easy way to sum up postgame exits: When the final horn sounds, get out of there! Do not worry about where the basketball goes; it's not your responsibility. Jog to your locker room and avoid confrontations.

Stay away from the scorer's table; it's too easy to be a target of emotional coaches, players or fans. There's no need to watch the postgame handshake; it's not your responsibility. The quicker you're off the floor, the safer you will be.

Free Throw Coverage (4-2)

The trail watches players on the opposite lane line (closer to the lead) except the opposite low block area. The trail also watches the free thrower.

The positioning means better coverage of the low-block area opposite the trail.

In MechaniGram 4-2, the lead looks opposite and watches ③, ③, ⑤ and ④, plus ⑤ nearest the lead. The trail looks opposite and watches ② and ④, plus free thrower ①. The trail's sec-

ondary coverage includes all the players behind the free-throw line extended.

As a point of emphasis, you should look for defensive players using hands or arms to disconcert the free thrower. Warn the players to prevent such actions, if you can. If the defender's actions warrant a violation, award a substitute free throw if the charity toss is missed. If that doesn't stop the illegal actions, use the technical foul. □

4-2

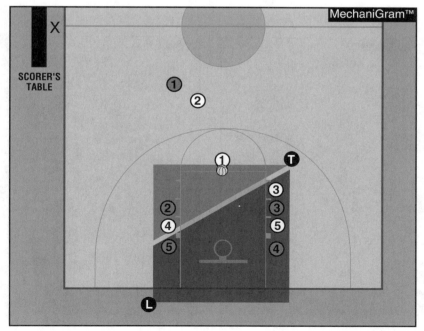

Free Throws: Trail Movement (4-3)

Do not come into the lane to administer the free throw; the lead administers all free throws.

Pick up the visible 10-second count with the arm furthest from the basket (PlayPic 4-3A). Using your outside arm ensures the arm movement doesn't distract the shooter and shows the count clearly to bench personnel, etc. When showing a visible count as a trail during a free-throw attempt, the count should be less demonstrative than your normal visible count so as to not distract the shooter and draw unnecessary attention to the official.

On the last free throw, use the "stop the clock" signal with open hand raised directly above the head immediately after the shooter releases the shot (PlayPic 4-3B). Use the same arm (furthest from the basket) to ensure the timer clearly sees the signal. During the flight of the try and with your arm still raised, penetrate slightly toward the endline using a two-step crossover move. That movement ensures good angles on rebounding action. If the shot is good, lower your arm. If the shot is no good and the ball is to remain live, use the "start the clock" signal as soon as the ball is touched by or touches a player.

There is no need to signal a made free throw. □

4-3A

4-3B

Notes

5 Throw-ins

Efficient movement and strong communication by the officials gets the ball back in play quickly and correctly.

> Officials may **bounce or hand the ball to the thrower.** The bounce to the thrower-in should only occur from the sideline or the backcourt endline.

> The thrower shall be **between the trail and the frontcourt basket.**

> When the trail administers the throw-in in the backcourt, the **thrower is always between the trail and the thrower's goal.**

> Depending on backcourt pressure, **the lead is positioned near the division line on the sideline opposite the trail,** ensuring both sidelines and both endlines are covered.

> If the throw-in is to be taken on the lead's sideline above the free-throw line extended, **the lead becomes the new trail and the trail becomes the new lead.**

> Before handing or bouncing the ball to the thrower, **tell the players the ball is about to become live** with short commands, like "ready" or "play it."

> Take at least **one step laterally away from the thrower** so your field of vision increases.

CHECK LIST

✔ Step away from thrower

✔ Use strong signals

✔ Use your voice

✔ Box in

Count shoulder high so all can see it, like Joe Bauer, Indianapolis, does here.

JIM WHITE

Administering a Throw-in (5-1)

On all throw-ins, the officials use the boxing-in method. Officials may bounce or hand the ball to the thrower. The bounce to the thrower-in should only occur from the sideline or the backcourt endline.

To ensure proper court coverage when handing the ball to the thrower, use the inside hand. Before handing or bouncing the ball to the thrower, tell the players to ball is about to become live with short commands, like "ready" or "play it." That gives all players a fair start. Then the administering official must move away from the thrower. Staying too close to the thrower obscures court vision. Move for proper angles to avoid straightlining. Take at least one step laterally away from the thrower so your field of vision increases. You should also step back from the endline or sideline, increasing visual clearance and assuring proper perspective.

In PlayPic 5-1A, the official hands the ball to the thrower with the hand closest to the thrower. In PlayPic 5-1B, the official steps away from the thrower and begins the throw-in count. The count is silent.

The step away from the thrower allows the official to see the thrower and provides a better angle on the players jockeying for position. □

Boxing-in Method When Trail Administers in Frontcourt (5-2)

When the trail administers the throw-in, the thrower is always between the trail and the frontcourt basket.

5-1A

5-1B

Under NFHS mechanics, the old lead is responsible for out-of-bounds calls along the sideline where the ball went out. Since the ball is being taken out above the free-throw line extended, the lead would move to new trail, while the trail would move to new lead. □

Trail Administers Above Free-throw Line Extended (5-3)

The NFHS manual states, "In the frontcourt, the throw-in is administered by the official responsible for the boundary where the throw in occurs." The manual also states the lead has the entire sideline on the lead side of the court. *Referee* recommends that, in most situations, the trail administers all throw-ins that occur above the free-throw line extended on either side of the floor so the lead can watch off-ball.

Coverage problems occur on plays that go out-of-bounds above the free-throw line extended and opposite the trail. If the trail is watching the player with the ball and the lead is watching the sideline above the free-throw line extended to see if the player violates, who is watching the rest of the players? No one.

Referee recommends that the

5-2

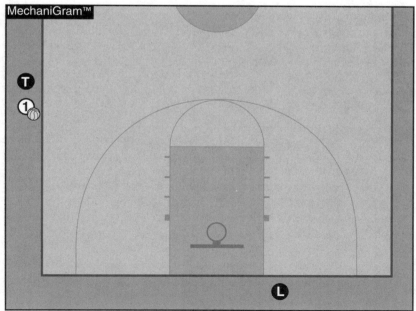

trail has sideline responsibility above the free-throw line extended and opposite the trail. Although counter to standard NFHS mechanics, that coverage recommendation extends to the ensuing throw-in. Since the trail is already watching the action near the sideline above the free-throw line extended, the trail administers the throw-in if the play remains in the frontcourt. The benefits: The lead can focus on watching off-ball and the ball is put back in play quickly.

In MechaniGram 5-3, the trail has moved beyond the center of the court to watch ① with the ball above the free-throw line

extended. ② knocks the ball out-of-bounds. The lead is watching off-ball. When the trail administers the throw-in from the sideline, the lead will move toward the opposite sideline to employ boxing in principles.

The NFHS manual clearly states that the official responsible for the sideline administers the throw-in. That means the lead would make the out-of-bounds call, then move up the sideline and administer the throw-in, becoming the new trail. The trail would move down to the endline and become the new lead.

If your state or local association follow the NFHS manual exclu-

5-3

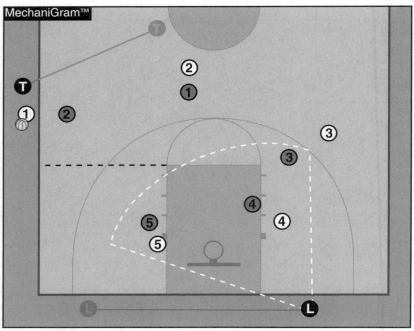

sively, do it. Check with the appropriate authorities to see if you can use the *Referee* recommendation. Be sure to discuss it thoroughly in your pregame conference with your partner. ☐

Running the endline (5-4)

If the player may run the endline, tell the thrower that before handing over the ball. Say something like, "You can run it," so the player knows of the option. It's also a good idea to wave your arm in front of you parallel to the endline (similar to a three-second call signal but with your arm swinging parallel to the endline). That shows everyone you've told the player it is not a designated-spot throw-in (again, you'll be seen on video handling it correctly). ☐

Do Not Break The Plane (5-5)

When a defensive player is guarding the throw-in closely and is positioned very close to the boundary line, use preventive officiating. Before handing the ball to the thrower, tell the defensive player to avoid a violation and not break the plane of the boundary line. It's a good idea to hold your hand up, using a stop sign signal, over the boundary line plane while talking to the player. That shows everyone you've warned the player not to violate (and it's on video). ☐

5-4

5-5

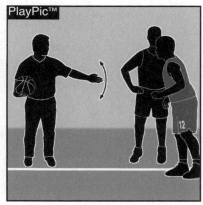

6 Transitions

The trail must react quickly to transitions play – without sacrificing good coverage. When in doubt, stay put.

> When an offensive violation occurs in your coverage area, **stop the clock,** signal the violation and the direction, then point to the spot for the throw-in.

> On occasion, the **trail may cut across the court** when moving to lead. It saves time and allows your partner to put the ball in play quickly.

> When an offensive player has the ball on the side of the floor opposite the trail, the trail must **move away from the near sideline** and get proper angles.

> The **same pass/crash principles** that apply in the lane area apply all over the court.

> The bump-and-run serves two main purposes: The trail official has a better chance of avoiding problems near the violation and the officials **move into place quicker** and get the ball live faster.

> Stay deep. **Avoid moving straight toward the play** because you could interfere with the play by stepping into a passing lane.

CHECK LIST

✔ Move off the sideline in the backcourt

✔ Watch for defensive pressure

✔ Aggressively take the crash

✔ Maintain eye contact with your partner

Look backward and don't backpedal, as David Gerletti, Pasadena, Calif., does here.

BOB MESSINA

The 'Bump-and-Run' (6-1)

The bump-and-run is a mechanic used by two-person crews to move swiftly from the frontcourt after a violation.

As the trail official, when an offensive violation occurs in your coverage area, stop the clock, signal the violation and the direction, then point to the spot for the throw-in. Next — after checking that there are no problems — sprint down court while viewing the action behind you and become the new lead official.

If you're the lead, eye the trail's signals, move toward the spot for the throw-in and administer it. You have now become the new trail. The lead "bumps" the trail down court and the trail moving to lead "runs" the floor.

In MechaniGram 6-1, ① causes the ball to go out-of-bounds. The trail correctly stops the clock, signals a violation and the direction, then communicates the throw-in spot to the lead. The trail then moves down court and becomes the new lead.

On occasion, the trail may cut across the court when moving to lead. It saves time and allows your partner to put the ball in play quickly. Be careful, however; the trail-to-lead movement should not cut across the court if players are quickly moving down court because a collision may occur. Whether you remain near the sideline or cut across the court, the new lead's field of vision must

6-1

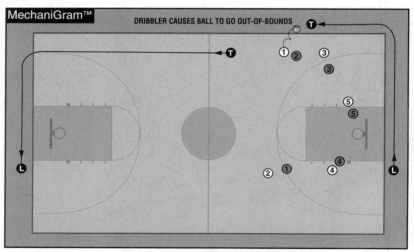

MechaniGram™   DRIBBLER CAUSES BALL TO GO OUT-OF-BOUNDS

keep players in sight — looking for potential problems — while moving down court. The new lead must balance the court on the throw-in and assume responsibility for the sideline opposite the throw-in.

The bump-and-run serves two main purposes: The trail official has a better chance of avoiding problems near the violation and the officials move into place quicker and get the ball live faster.

For example, in MechaniGram 6-1, the dribbler is unhappy because the dribbler thought there was a foul before turning the ball over. If the trail stood there to administer the throw-in and waited for the lead to get all the way down court, a heated conversation could occur simply because the official who made the call is still on the spot. The bump-and-run lets you clear the area and avoid unneeded and potentially damaging conversations.

Also, the bump-and-run gets the ball live faster. Again, if the trail stayed put and administered the throw-in, the lead would have to run the length of the floor before the trail could hand the ball to the thrower. That's a long time even if the lead is fast! The bump-and-run cuts the distance each official travels and gets the game going smoothly, allowing the crew to establish and maintain a quality tempo. □

REFEREE

Try This

"The trail wants to get into position for their primary match up as well as seeing the other eight players. Don't over run the play, if you're ahead of the ball and looking back at it, you can't see the other players. Stay back."

— Ed Rush
NBA Director of Officiating

Transition: Trail Movement Off Sideline (6-2)

Effective two-person court coverage requires significant movement by the trail off the sideline. The same philosophies are true in the transition game when play is moving from the backcourt to the frontcourt.

When an offensive player has the ball on the side of the floor opposite the trail, the trail must move away from the near sideline and get proper angles. By staying too close to the near sideline, the trail cannot effectively see action near the ball and must make judgments from a distance — way too far to convince anyone the trail saw the play correctly.

In MechaniGram 6-2, ① dribbles the ball upcourt opposite the new trail as ① applies defensive pressure. The rest of the players are advancing to the frontcourt as the new lead watches off-ball. To see the play well, the new trail must move far off the near sideline and work to get a good angle.

Stay deep. Avoid moving straight toward the play because you could interfere with the play by stepping into a passing lane. Take an angle toward the backcourt endline to decrease your chances of interfering with the play.

By moving off the sideline and angling toward the play, you're in a much better position to see the play. ☐

6-2

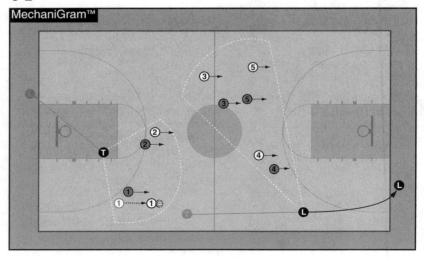

MechaniGram™

Pass/crash during transition (6-3)

The same pass/crash principles that apply in the lane area apply all over the court. One trouble spot for officials is the pass/crash when a team in transition starts a break up the court. Many times you'll see players leave their feet to make a pass then crash into defenders. Block? Charge? No-call?

In MechaniGram 6-3, ④ rebounds and throws an outlet pass to a streaking ①. ① catches the pass and dribbles up court trying to start a fastbreak. ③ is filling the passing lane down the center of the court.

② steps in to stop ① from advancing into the frontcourt.

① leaps into the air and passes to ③. ① then crashes into ②.

The lead must quickly read the fastbreak and move toward the sideline to become the new trail. There the new trail has a good look at ① leaping, passing and crashing. □

6-3

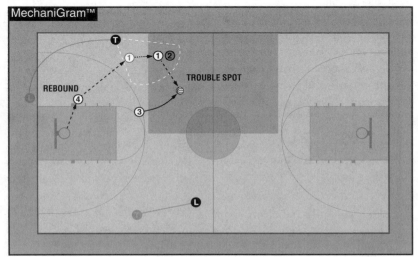

Don't Blow It!

Six Tips on Using Your Whistle

When most people consider communicating, they think of talking. There are many other ways to communicate — like body language and signals — that you use every time you're on the court. One tool that you use that doesn't always get a lot of consideration is your whistle. It is a very important part of communication.

Think of the whistle as a communication tool. It's really just an extension of your voice and your signals. Blowing the whistle loudly has the same impact of you screaming; blowing the whistle softly equates to whispering. A "normal" whistle blow is as if you were talking in a normal tone of voice.

Use these six tips on blowing the whistle and you will be more effective.

1. Sharp Blast When Stopping the Clock

When stopping the clock (using either the open-hand or closed-fist overhead signals),

simultaneously use a sharp, strong whistle blast. There's no need to blow the whistle many times with short blasts; that doesn't communicate anything of substance and draws unnecessary attention to the call. Officials who blow the whistle many times while making a single call are generally showboating. It's not needed.

2. Substitutions: Do What Your Supervisor Wants

Blowing the whistle while beckoning in a substitute is debatable. Some supervisors want officials to blow their whistle when beckoning A substitutes. Why? The whistle gets the attention of the substitute and the official's partner, letting both know the substitution is taking place.

Other supervisors don't want officials blowing the whistle when beckoning in substitutes. Why? Blowing the whistle is demonstrative and draws attention to the official. Plus, with good signals and eve contact, the whistle isn't needed.

Here might be the most obvious *Referee* recommendation we've published in awhile: Do what your supervisor wants. If there is no supervisor or no decision on what method to use, Referee recommends blowing the whistle only when there is so some confusion as to when the substitute may enter or when the substitute can't hear your voice or see your I signals. On most substitutions, it's not necessary to blow the whistle.

3. Use a Longer Whistle on Timeouts.

When a team requests and is granted a timeout, use a slightly longer whistle while signaling the timeout. That longer whistle distinguishes a timeout from a normal whistle blast that stops the clock.

4. Slow Down on Double-whistles.

Some plays have both officials briefly watching the same player. That's especially true with on-ball coverage in a halfcourt setting in the lane area. Sometimes both officials blow the whistle at the same time. By following the cor-

rect procedure, you'll avoid the embarrassment and confusion of having one official signaling one thing and the other signaling something else at the same time.

There's a general rule for double-whistles: If the play is moving toward you, you have the call. If the play is moving away from you, you give the call up to your partner.

Following correct signal procedures is critical with double-whistles. If you don't, you'll probably have an unwanted double call. It's important to take the time to use the correct, signal to stop the clock (either open hand or fist overhead, depending on the call) and simultaneously blow your whistle. If you hear your partner's whistle, quickly make eye contact before signaling anything else. You and your partner will likely need to penetrate on the play and quickly tell each other what you've got. Again, in most cases, the official who the play is moving toward likely takes the call.

An exception is if the official who has the play moving away has a foul or violation that occurred before the partner's whistle.

Understand that most double

whistles occur in the lane area. When you make a call in that area, expect that there might be a double whistle and quickly glance at your partner before signaling the type of foul or violation. Knowing where double whistles tend to occur helps when you can't hear your partner's whistle because of crowd noise or the noise of your own whistle.

Disciplined signals, good eve contact and verbal communication eliminate double calls on double whistles.

5. Blow it Louder To Help Sell a Call.

Use your whistle to your advantage. Think of it as an extension of your voice. Blow it louder than normal when you really need to sell something. Use a strong, short blast in most situations.

6. A Soft Whistle Means a Soft Call.

Avoid blowing a soft whistle. just like soft signals that aren't crisp and clear, soft whistles convey that you're not sure about what you've called. Make sure your whistle blasts exude confidence and control without going overboard. □

Notes

8 Postgame Review

After the game, it's a good idea to review what happened during the game. The postgame review is another important part of the learning process.

The first order of business immediately after the game is to relax. Officiating can be stressful and postgame relaxation helps get you back to normal.

At a reasonable time after the game, review the game with your partner. Some like to review before taking a shower and relaxing. Others like to wait until the postgame dinner. Do whatever is convenient and comfortable for you and your partner.

When reviewing the game, talk about:

Points of Emphasis

Were the pregame points of emphasis handled effectively. Many times, rough play is emphasized. Did you control the game effectively? Were off-ball fouls called appropriately? If the points of emphasis were not handled properly, discuss remedies for your next game.

Tempo

Did you let the game come to you or did you assert yourself when you didn't need to? Did the game develop a flow? If not, is there anything you could have done to keep the game moving? Did you get the ball back in play quickly without rushing?

Bench Decorum

How did you handle the benches? Did you let the coaches go too far? Were you approachable?

Strange Plays, Rulings

Discuss and review any strange plays or rulings. If necessary, confirm your ruling with the rulebook and casebook. Make sure you've got the rule down so you can apply it correctly if it happens again.

Solicit Constructive Criticism

One of the ways to improve is to get opinions and advice from others. Your partner is a great source. Always ask if there's anything you could have done differently or better.

After asking, accept the constructive criticism. Don't be one of those referees that asks, "How'd I do?" expecting a shower of praise. If you don't want to know the truth, don't ask. Take the criticism offered, analyze the comments and apply the changes if you feel it's appropriate.

Be ready to offer a critique when asked. It's frustrating for an official who wants to learn to invite criticism only to hear, "You did a good job." There must be something that needs improving! You ought to be able to give your partner at least three things to think about after every game.

Write a Journal

Consider keeping a journal during your season. Write down strange plays, your feelings about your performance, notes about your partner, things you did well and things you can improve on. The journal is a great way to look back during and after the season to see if there are patterns. If the same things keep appearing in your journal, you know there are things that need to be addressed.

Reviewing the journal is also a great way to start thinking about officiating before next season. □

All Sports

All Levels

Always

There For You

NASO

The National Association of Sports Officials

- NASO's "Members Only Edition" of *Referee* magazine every month. Members receive 96-pages of *Referee* with 16-pages of association news, "members only" tips, case plays and ducational product discounts.

- Members receive a *FREE* educational publication valued up to $9.95.

- Discounts on NASO/*Referee* publications such as the Officials' Guidebooks, rules comparisons and sport-specific preseason publications make you a better official.

- Referral service in the event you move to another community.

- Web page and e-mail communications keep you updated on NASO news, services and benefits.

- "Ask Us" rules interpretations service.

- Sports-specific rules quizzes.

- Free NASO e-mail address.

- Free access to the *NASO LockerRoom* — an NASO cyberspace service.

- Membership Certificate and laminated membership card.

- NASO Code of Ethics.

For a complete brochure and membership information contact:
NASO • 2017 Lathrop Avenue • Racine, WI 53405
262/632-5448 • 262/632-5460 (fax)
naso@naso.org or visit our website at www.naso.org